Bran Castle

by Grace Hansen

Abdo Kids
FAMOUS CASTLES

Abdo Kids Jumbo is an Imprint of Abdo Kids
abdobooks.com

abdobooks.com

Published by Abdo Kids, a division of ABDO, P.O. Box 398166, Minneapolis, Minnesota 55439.

Printed in the United States of America, North Mankato, Minnesota.

052021

092021

THIS BOOK CONTAINS
RECYCLED MATERIALS

Photo Credits: Granger Collection, iStock, Shutterstock

Production Contributors: Teddy Borth, Jennie Forsberg, Grace Hansen
Design Contributors: Candice Keimig, Pakou Moua

Library of Congress Control Number: 2020947526

Publisher's Cataloging-in-Publication Data

Names: Hansen, Grace, author.

Title: Bran castle / by Grace Hansen

Description: Minneapolis, Minnesota : Abdo Kids, 2022 | Series: Famous castles | Includes online resources and index.

Identifiers: ISBN 9781098207281 (lib. bdg.) | ISBN 9781098208127 (ebook) | ISBN 9781098208547 (Read-to-Me ebook)

Subjects: LCSH: Castelul Bran (Bran, Brașov, Romania)--Juvenile literature. | Castles--Juvenile literature. | Architecture--Juvenile literature.

Classification: DDC 728.81--dc23

Table of Contents

Bran Castle

Bran Castle is in the small town of Bran in Romania. The **gothic** castle sits on a steep cliff. It looks over Bran and the most important **medieval trade route**.

Europe
Bran
Romania

On November 19, 1377, the Hungarian King Louis the Great issued a document. It gave the people of Brasov the honor of building a stone castle. The castle was complete in 1388.

King Louis the Great

The castle sat in an important place. It was high enough to watch for enemies like the Turks from the **Ottoman Empire**. It was also on a vital **trade route**.

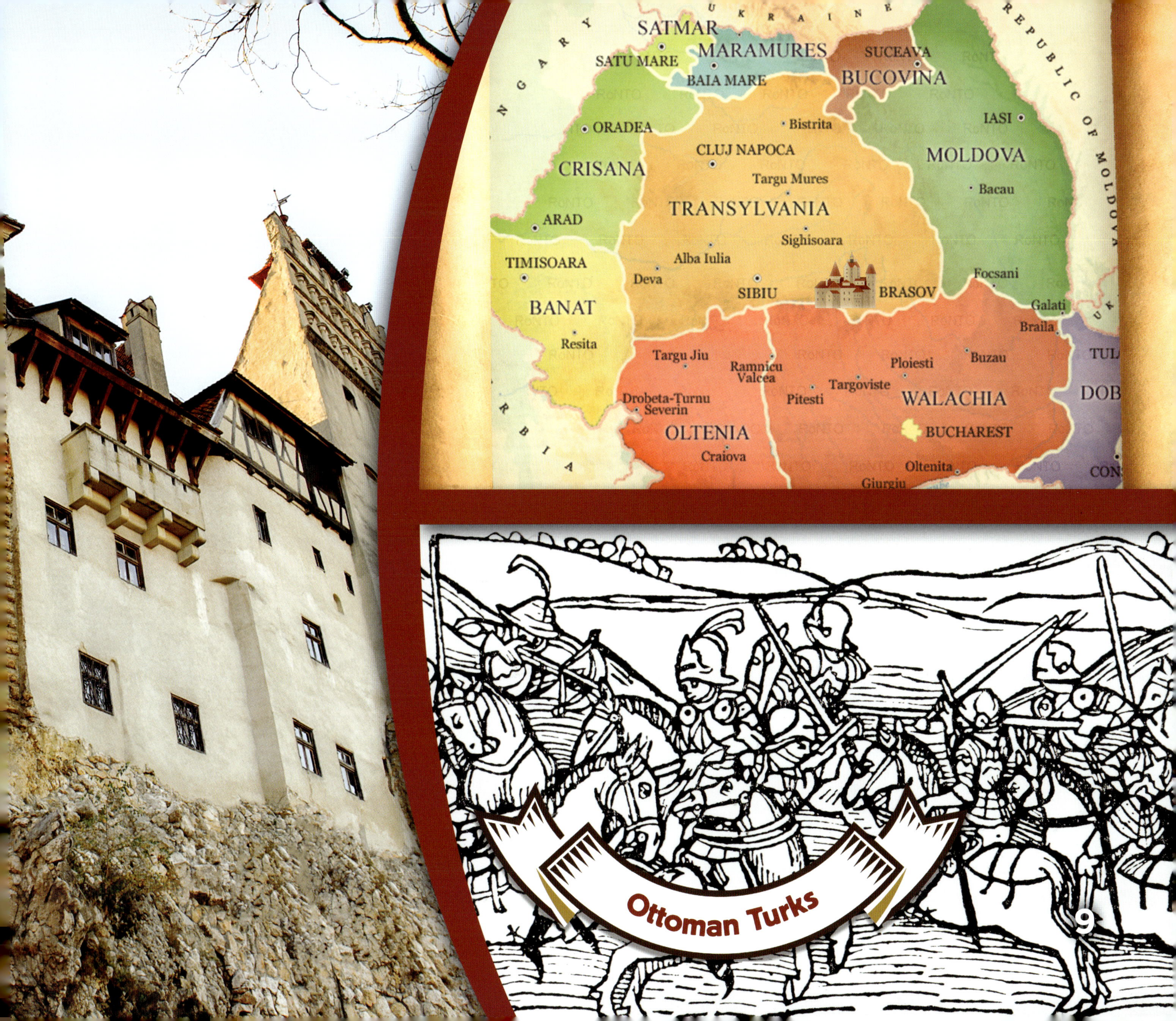
UKRAINE
REPUBLIC OF MOLDOVA
SATMAR
SATU MARE
MARAMURES
BAIA MARE
SUCEAVA
BUCOVINA
ORADEA
Bistrita
IASI
CLUJ NAPOCA
CRISANA
MOLDOVA
Targu Mures
Bacau
ARAD
TRANSYLVANIA
Sighisoara
TIMISOARA
Alba Iulia
Deva
Focsani
SIBIU
BRASOV
BANAT
Galati
Braila
Resita
Targu Jiu
Ramnicu Valcea
Ploiesti
Buzau
Targoviste
Drobeta-Turnu Severin
Pitesti
WALACHIA
OLTENIA
BUCHAREST
Craiova
Oltenita
Giurgiu
Ottoman Turks

The castle served a military role. It also held goods that moved in and out of Transylvania. Soldiers and others lived in the castle.

By 1836, the castle had lost its importance. Bran was no longer a military or trade point. But nearly 100 years later, the castle was given a new purpose.

A New Purpose

In 1920, the people of Brasov gifted the castle to Queen Marie of Romania. Bran Castle became her favorite place to live. The castle was **renovated** by 1932. It was now fit for a queen.

Queen Marie

In 1938, Queen Marie died. She left the castle to Princess Ileana. A **Communist Party** took over the area in 1948. Ileana was forced out of the castle and the country.

Queen Marie
Princess Ileana

The Castle Today

In 2006, Romania gave the castle back to the royal family. The beautifully **renovated** castle reopened in June 2009. Today visitors can explore its 57 rooms and secret passageways.

The castle holds and protects Queen Marie's art and furniture. It also displays **medieval** weapons and clothing.

More Facts

- The main secret passageway in Bran connects the first floor to the third floor. It would have been used in emergencies to escape the castle. The entrance was hidden by a fireplace.

- The castle is spooky to some people. This is because some relate it to Bram Stoker's horror novel *Dracula*.

- Because of his name, some people also relate the castle to Vlad III Dracula. Vlad was a Romanian ruler in the 1400s. He was known to be a cruel murderer. However, most historians agree that the book, the man, and the castle are mostly unrelated.

Glossary

Communist Party – in Romania, the Socialist Republic of Romania that existed officially from 1947 to 1989. Communism is a system in which everything is owned by the government and given to people as needed.

gothic – of or relating to the style of architecture characterized by its pointed arches and ribbed vaults.

medieval – of or having to do with the Middle Ages, a period of European history from about 500 CE to 1500 CE.

Ottoman Empire – an empire created by Turkish tribes that grew to be very powerful during the 15th and 16th centuries.

renovate – to put in good condition by repairing, remodeling, or the like.

trade route – a route followed by people who sell and buy goods.

Index

Visit abdokids.com to access crafts, games, videos, and more!

Use Abdo Kids code **FBK7281** or scan this QR code!